First-Place Reading

PHONICS PRACTICE READER

GRADE 1

Copyright © by Harcourt, Inc.

All rights reserved. No part of this publication may be reproduced or transmitted in any form or by any means, electronic or mechanical, including photocopy, recording, or any information storage and retrieval system, without permission in writing from the publisher.

Requests for permission to make copies of any part of the work should be addressed to School Permissions and Copyrights, Harcourt, Inc., 6277 Sea Harbor Drive, Orlando, Florida 32887-6777. Fax: 407-345-2418.

HARCOURT and the Harcourt Logo are trademarks of Harcourt, Inc., registered in the United States of America and/or other jurisdictions.

Printed in the United States of America

ISBN 0-15-334593-4

2 3 4 5 6 7 8 9 10   179   10 09 08 07 06 05 04 03 02

CONTENTS

Burt Bird and His Friends . . 5
Phonic Element: /ûr/ *er, ir, ur*

Oat Muffins 13
Phonic Element: /ō/ *ow, oa*

Who Dove in Blue Cove . . 21
Phonic Element: /ō/ *o-e, o*

CONTENTS

Dave and Kate **29**
Phonic Element: /ā/ a-e, ai, ay

Whiskers at Sea **37**
Phonic Element: /hw/ wh

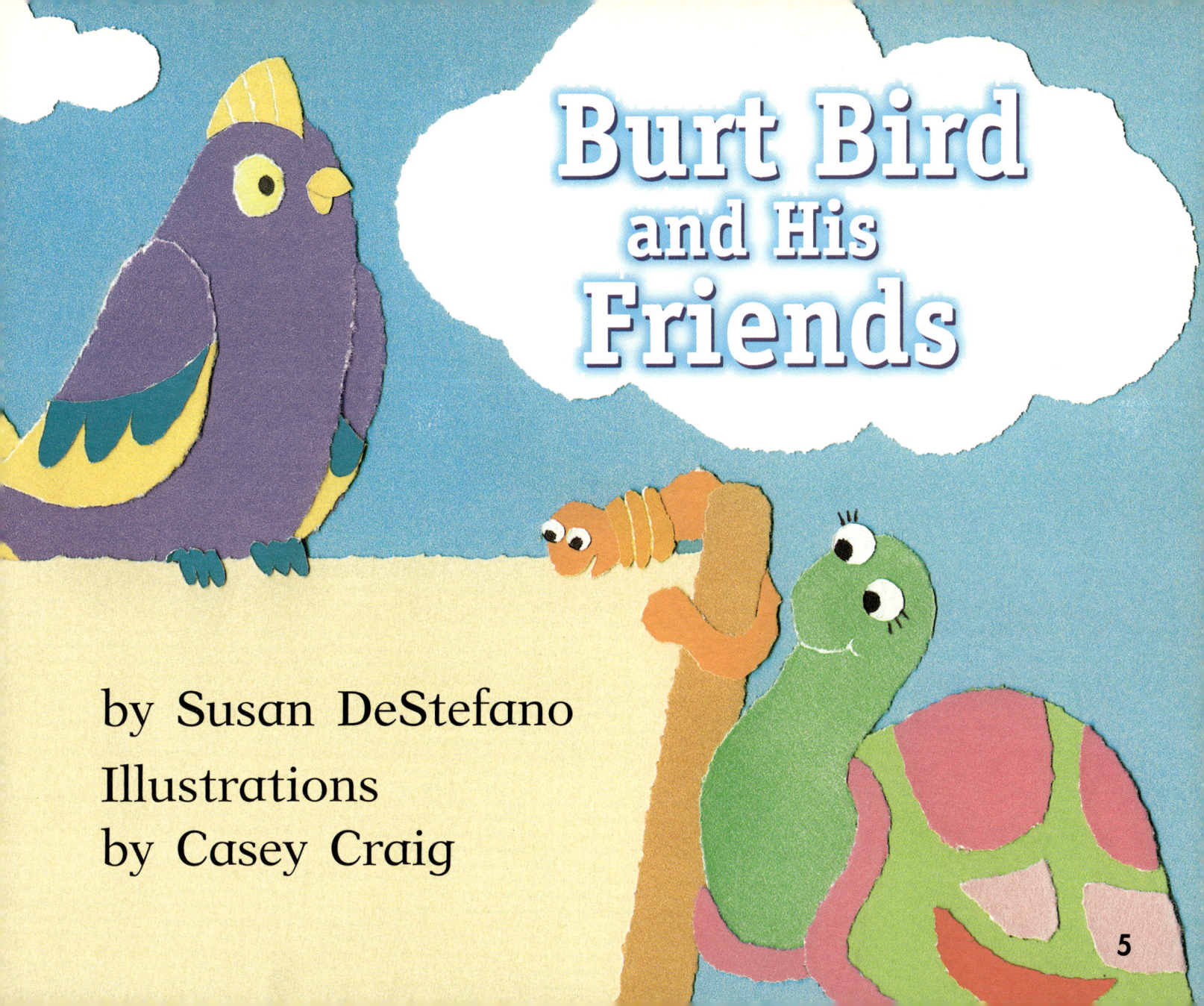

Burt Bird and His Friends

by Susan DeStefano
Illustrations by Casey Craig

I am Burt Bird. I perch and chirp. I fly all about looking for things to eat.

All birds must eat a lot.
Sometimes I eat so much
I think I'll just burst!

This is my
friend Gert Turtle.
Her shell is her home.
Hello, Gert! Come out!

A turtle's shell is a very good home. It's very hard. Not much can hurt Gert!

Let's turn by this plant.
This is my friend Kirk.
He's curled up in the dirt.

Kirk lives in the dirt. He even eats dirt! Kirk digs in and stirs things up.

Kirk, Gert, and I all see this garden in a different way.

OAT MUFFINS

by William Henry
Illustrations by Alexi Natchev

Two little goats trot down the road. "Sniff, sniff! Muffins!"

"Oh, no!" Toad moans and groans. "The goats will eat all my muffins!"

Toad gets a bowl. She shows the goats how to make their own oat muffins.

"Have fun, fellows!" Toad croaks as the goats go home. "Do not forget the oats."

The goats dump the oats into a bowl. They mix in other stuff, too.
  Soap!
  Toast!
  Coal!
  An old coat!
They stir the stuff faster and faster!

"Our muffins are so good!" boast the goats. "They are the sweetest of all!"

Who Dove in Blue Cove?

by Lester Johnson   Illustrated by Jackie Snider

This is Blue Cove. Who dove in Blue Cove? Come close and let's go see!

This is a hermit crab. He chose a new home. It looks like a stone.

Those are sharks. I think they are napping. Let's let them doze!

Whales are very big sea animals.
They don't have gills like fish.
They have a blowhole.

That's a sawfish. Did it use its nose to poke all those holes in that boat? No, but a close look at its teeth shows how the sawfish got its name.

Now you have seen Blue Cove.
Who dove in Blue Cove? You did!

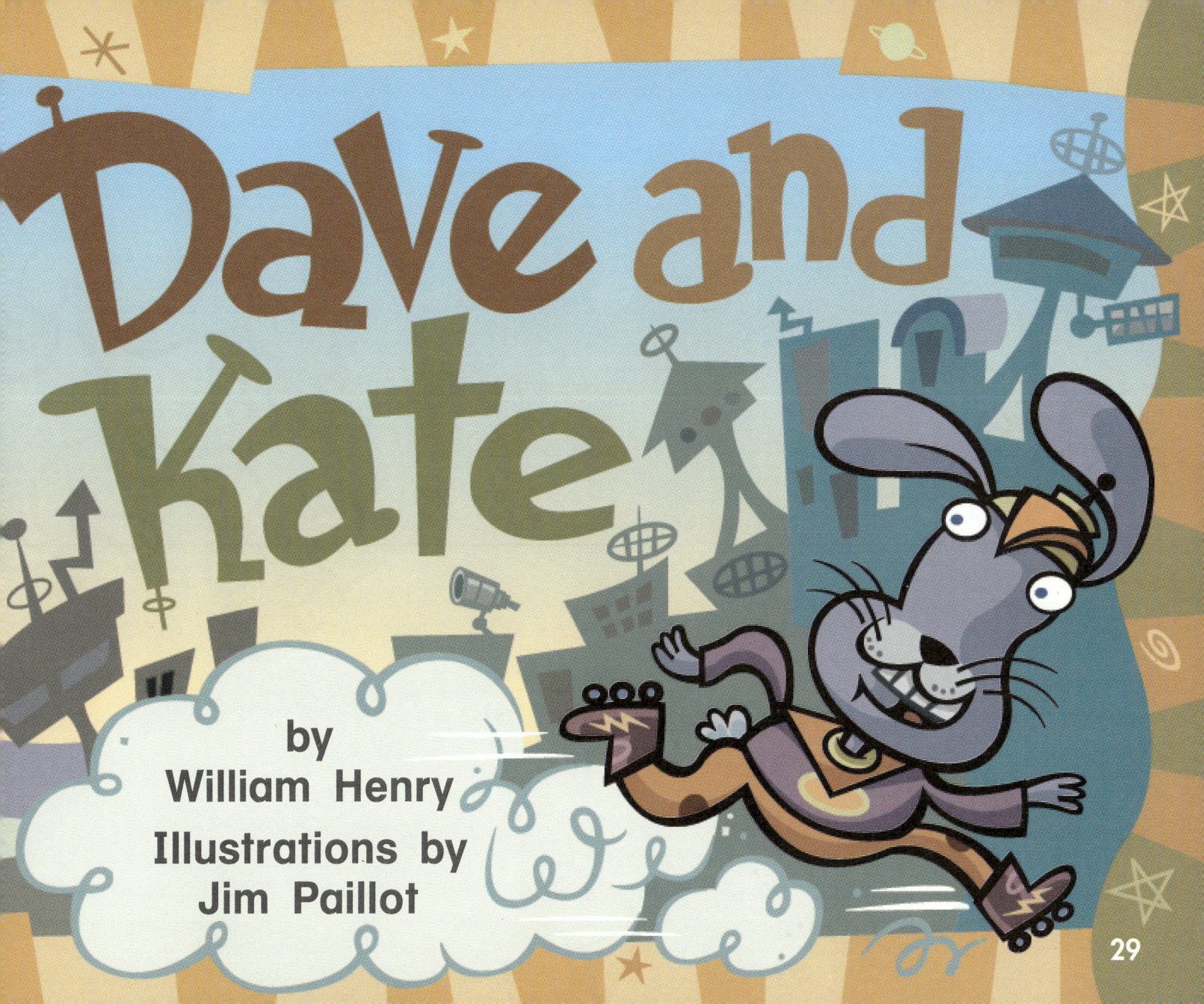

Dave Rabbit was never late. He would speed up the lane on his skates.

Kate Turtle would take her time.
Dave would always wave to Kate.

One day, Dave came up with a game. "Kate," he said, "let's have a contest. The first one to skate to the lake wins." Kate didn't think she could win, but she gave it a try.

"Kate's so slow," said Dave.
"I should take a rest. I'll still win!"
Dave ate some grapes. Then he
had a nap in the shade. Kate
never gave up. She came creeping
by on her slow, slow skates.

Dave was much too late. Kate was the winner. She came in first at the lake!

Whiskers at Sea

by Nancy Chiong

Illustrations by Steve Royal

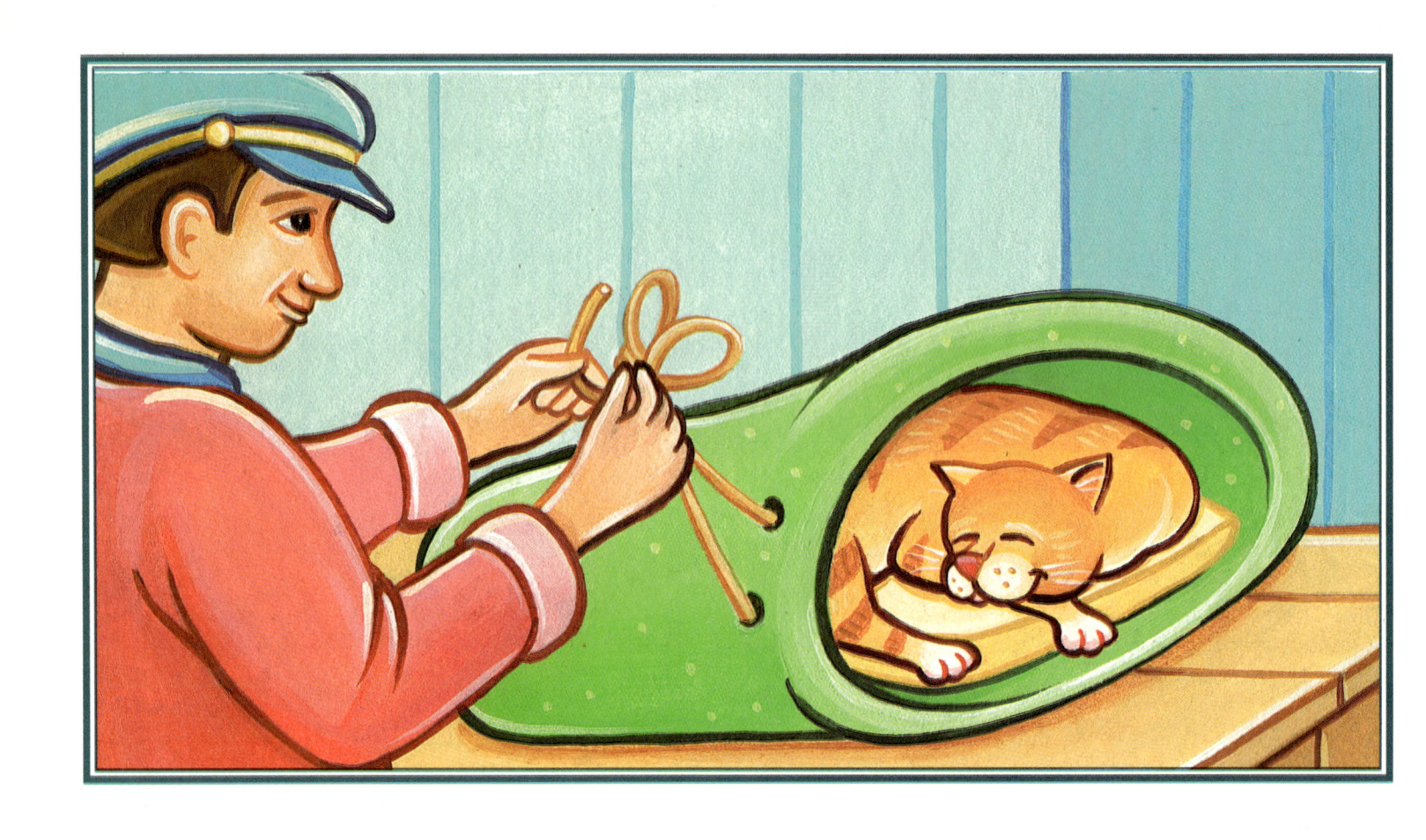

Whiskers likes to nap. Once she finds a good spot, she snuggles up.

Where in the world is Whiskers now?
She's going out to sea!

A man turns a big wheel. Which way will the boat go? Further out to sea!

"Look," a girl whispers to her dad. "A cat! I thought we came to see whales!"

Whir! Whish! Whirl! Is it the wind?
Is the wind whipping up the waves?

No, it's a whale! Everyone watches—everyone but Whiskers.

Whiskers didn't see any whales,
but she had a whale of a nap!